A Walk Thru the Book of

ESTHER

Courage in the Face of Crisis

Walk Thru the Bible

BakerBooks

a division of Baker Publishing Group
Grand Rapids, Michigan

© 2010 by Walk Thru the Bible

Published by Baker Books
a division of Baker Publishing Group
P.O. Box 6287, Grand Rapids, MI 49516-6287
www.bakerbooks.com

Printed in the United States of America

Library of Congress Cataloging-in-Publication Data
A walk thru the book of Esther : courage in the face of crisis / Walk Thru the Bible.
    p. cm.
    Includes bibliographical references (p.   ).
    ISBN 978-0-8010-7180-5 (pbk.)
    1. Bible. O.T. Esther—Textbooks. 2. Esther, Queen of Persia. I. Walk Thru the Bible (Educational ministry)
    BS1375.55.W36 2010
    222'.907—dc22   2009046941

10 11 12 13 14 15 16   7 6 5 4 3 2 1

Contents

Introduction

Sometimes you think your steps are being guided by an unseen hand. You don't know exactly what the future holds, but where you've been makes sense as a setup to where you think you're going. Your life seems to have a rhyme and a reason.

Then there are those times when nothing makes sense. The twists and turns of life have taken you off course, if there ever was a course to begin with. As far as you can tell, there is neither rhyme nor reason in your steps. Maybe you're headed somewhere specific, but the road to get there is anything but a direct route.

Who is pulling the strings of your life? Are you being tossed around by random circumstances, or are your steps predetermined by divine will? Are you subject to chance coincidences or bound by fate? Or, to put it in more theological terms, is your life a product of free will—yours and others'—or a product of a sovereign plan?

There's always tension between the seemingly random events of life and the overall purposes of God, both in the big picture of history and the personal picture of your own story. Philosophers and theologians argue the nuances of how these things fit together, but Scripture doesn't spell it all out for us. It lets us experience our world and interact with God as we walk through it, trusting him to guide us where he wants us to go. We have choices along the way, but we also have a purpose to fulfill. Only he knows exactly how our choices blend with his will.

While the book of Esther doesn't answer all those questions, it certainly addresses them. The book tells a story of the preservation of God's people by an unseen (and unmentioned) hand. The Jews in this story are in the Persian capital, having been dispersed by the Babylonian captivity almost a century earlier. They become the targets of a kingdom-wide plot and are dramatically delivered. The reader is left to decide whether or not God has been orchestrating events, though the remarkable "coincidences" and plot twists seem to make it clear that someone is protecting these Jews. Even though they are scattered throughout the Persian Empire, most of them far from the land of God's promise, they are still under heaven's watchful eye.

The Setting

Jews from the southern kingdom of Judah had been taken into captivity by the Babylonian Empire over a twelve-year period culminating with the destruction of the temple in 586 BC. After Persia overthrew Babylon several decades later, Persian king Cyrus the Great issued a decree in 537 allowing Jews to return to Jerusalem. Many did, but most remained scattered across the empire. Cyrus was succeeded by Cambyses, then Darius, and then Xerxes (aka Ahasuerus), the king in the book of Esther. Xerxes ruled from 485 until 465, when he was assassinated by one of his advisors. He seems to have had an enormous desire for personal glory that sent him off on an ambitious (and failed) campaign against the Greeks. This fits well with his portrayal in Esther 1 as a king who loved to have lavish banquets in his own honor. He was apparently not only demanding but also indecisive and overly dependent on advice from those around him, which explains how someone like Haman came to have so much authority. Xerxes is portrayed as a man of weak character with strong ambitions and the means to attain them.

The kingdom of Persia during the time of Xerxes stretched roughly from the modern-day border between Pakistan and India, to Bulgaria in Eastern Europe, and to Libya and northern Sudan in North Africa. Xerxes tried to expand further into Greek territories—the famous battle of Thermopylae was part of that campaign—but failed and returned to Susa, one of the four capitals of his empire. This is when most of the book of Esther (chapters 2–10) takes place. During this time, Jews were a very widespread minority throughout the empire.

History or Comedy?

Esther is full of what many people consider to be exaggerations and caricatures. There's a banquet that lasts six months. The writer mentions 127 Persian provinces, though Greek historians have recorded only twenty. The villain is ludicrously evil. The language is almost humorously repetitive (e.g., the order to "destroy, kill and annihilate" all the Jews). The misunderstandings between Xerxes and Haman would fit well in a slapstick comedy. And a seventy-five-foot gallows is erected in a city in which the tallest buildings are about thirty feet high. But the story can have an entirely different feel depending on the perspective of the reader. A six-month-long banquet could be a kingdom-wide "open house" of the palace rather than an event attended by guests in its entirety, or it could be a planning session among nobles to

prepare for the upcoming Greek war. The writer could be refer-
ring to smaller subsections of provinces than Greek historians
did. Villains as evil as Haman have existed in this world; sometimes even repeated or exaggerated words aren't strong enough
to capture a thought; gross misunderstandings do happen; and
enormous instruments of torture and death have been built. There
is no compelling reason to conclude that Esther must have been
a play, an allegory, or comic fiction. It is presented as a story of
God's people in a specific place at a specific time.

Themes

Several prominent themes are woven throughout the book of
Esther:

- *The sovereignty of a God who is unnamed and behind the
  scenes but nonetheless faithful to his promises to his people.* In
  reading Esther and in our daily lives, we have to decide
  if God is behind the scenes or not. It isn't spelled out for
  us, either in the book or in our normal routines.
- *Feasts and fasts.* A flurry of feasting in chapter 1 is followed
  by a banquet in honor of the king's marriage to Esther; the
  king and his right-hand man sit down to eat and drink
  after making a horrendous decree; two banquets are offered
  by Esther to plead her case before Xerxes and Haman;
  and there is another flurry of feasting and celebrating at
  the end of the book as the holiday of Purim is established.
  But the frequent feasting is, by contrast, halted by a three-
  day fast in the middle of the story as the Jews prepare for
  Esther's intervention.
- *Boldness and faithfulness in a crisis.* Esther had to make
  a stand in spite of the potential consequences. She had

to decide whether to step forward in a crisis or shrink back from it. Her example serves as a challenge for us to recognize the position God has given us and to consider whether we are chosen "for such a time as this" in the crises we go through.

- *Turnabout.* As the story develops, a series of reversals culminates with Mordecai being exalted to a royal position and the Jews being able to plunder their enemies as decisively as their enemies had planned to destroy them. When 9:1 declares that "the tables were turned," it's highlighting a major theme of God's power to dramatically rearrange circumstances in our favor and for his purposes.

- *God's ability to use anyone.* In the world's chess match, God took a girl who thought she was a pawn, made her a queen, and used her to turn the course of a king.

- *God's ability to turn our apparent disasters into symbols of triumph.* The very instrument of destruction prepared for the Jews became the instrument on which their archenemy died.

- *The humble exalted and the proud made low.* The completely vulnerable and faithful people in Esther end up in positions of extreme security and power, while the arrogant enemies of God's people are humiliated.

- *Anti-Semitism.* The book of Esther is a story of Satan's perpetual hostility against the nation through whom God's revelation and the Messiah would come.

- *God's faithfulness to his promises.* Even though these Jews had decided not to return to the Promised Land, God zealously defended them anyway in their dispersion. He also fulfilled a centuries-old promise to wipe out one of Israel's enemies. He finishes the battles he starts.

How to Use This Guide

The discussion guides in this series are intended to create a link between past and present, between the cultural and historical context of the Bible and real life as we experience it today. By putting ourselves as closely into biblical situations as possible, we can begin to understand how God interacted with his people in the past and, therefore, how he interacts with us today. The information in this book makes ancient Scripture relevant to twenty-first-century life as God means for us to live it.

The questions in this book are geared to do what a discussion guide should do: provoke discussion. You won't see obvious "right" answers to most of these questions. That's because biblical characters had to wrestle with deep spiritual issues and didn't have easy, black-and-white answers handed to them. They discovered God's will as he led them and revealed himself to them—the same process we go through today, though we have the added help of their experiences to inform us. Biblical characters experienced God in complex situations, and so do we. By portraying those situations realistically, we learn how to apply the Bible to our own lives. One of the best ways to do that is through in-depth discussion with other believers.

The discussion questions within each session are designed to elicit every participant's input, regardless of his or her level of preparation. Obviously, the more group members prepare by reading the biblical text and the background information in the study guide, the more they will get out of it. But even in busy weeks that afford no preparation time, everyone will be able to participate in a meaningful way.

The discussion questions also allow your group quite a bit of latitude. Some groups prefer to briefly discuss the questions in order to cover as many as possible, while others focus only on one or two of them in order to have more in-depth conversations. Since this study is designed for flexibility, feel free to adapt it according to the personality and needs of your group.

Each session ends with a hypothetical situation that relates to the passage of the week. Discussion questions are provided, but group members may also want to consider role-playing the scenario or setting up a two-team debate over one or two of the questions. These exercises often cultivate insights that wouldn't come out of a typical discussion.

Regardless of how you use this material, the biblical text will always be the ultimate authority. Your discussions may take you to many places and cover many issues, but they will have the greatest impact when they begin and end with God's Word itself. And never forget that the Spirit who inspired the Word is in on the discussion too. May he guide it—and you— wherever he wishes.

The Vulnerable and the Invincible

ESTHER 1–2

The Jews of Europe didn't have their own army, their own economic system, or even their own country. They were scattered throughout communities, among various professions, and across borders. They were numerous but not organized, financially strong but not in control, integrated into society but, for the most part, not influential over it. In other words, they were vulnerable to the machinery of national governments and military force—sitting ducks on the European landscape.

By contrast, the German government was growing in power, and its military was known for its efficiency. The German economy was recovering from years of runaway inflation and extreme instability. A regional force was developing, though few in the late 1930s knew how much of a force German leaders wanted their country to be.

An overall anti-Semitic sentiment helped many political and economic leaders to magnify the "threat" Jews posed to German culture and social systems, but such fears were unfounded—a convenient excuse to turn hatred into national policy. Over time, that's exactly what happened in Germany and the countries conquered by Hitler. Lesser persecution of Jews turned into massive pogroms against them, eventually becoming the "final solution" that exterminated millions in concentration camps and shocked the world. In the showdown between social vulnerability and political dominance, dominance wreaked havoc for years.

The first two chapters of Esther also portray a vivid contrast between vulnerability and dominance. Persia's impressive wealth and power are on display as an impetuous king basks in the glory of his realm. Meanwhile, an orphaned girl is raised by her cousin in a Jewish subculture that was dispersed across the empire. This contrast will play out in dramatic and surprising ways as the book progresses, but the stage is set this way for a reason. The struggle between power and vulnerability will demonstrate in remarkable ways the invincibility of those whom God has chosen.

This theme is not unique to Jews living in powerful kingdoms. It's true for anyone who has been called by God to represent him in a hostile or overwhelming world. Like David against Goliath, Gideon against the Midianites, Daniel against the lions, or Christians against Roman paganism, we have complete authority to stand against a culture, a system, or an institution that opposes God. A single servant plus God always amounts to a majority. No matter the situation in life, our vulnerability is not an issue. We have the backing of a higher authority.

A WEDDING BANQUET?

Some have suggested that the seven-day banquet in Esther 1:5 that comes on the heels of the six-month feast may have been a wedding celebration for Xerxes and Vashti. If so, the request for the bride to make an appearance seems more reasonable than it would if the context was simply a male-dominated drinking party—though her refusal to come would make much less sense in that context. Regardless, Vashti apparently considered it to be a shameful request for an honorable Persian woman, so she did something the king considered even more shameful. She defied him.

It's important to remember that whether we're in a large-scale conflict with the culture or a smaller-scale conflict with illness or an overbearing to-do list, God supports his people and invites us to bring our weaknesses to him. In fact, he promises to be our strength in the midst of our weakness. Those who have been chosen and called by him have a powerful ally for life.

A Lavish Feast: Esther 1

For six months, Susa has hosted nobility and military leaders from across the Persian Empire who have come to see Xerxes' majesty. The display has been extravagant—wealth and opulence, feasting, a festival atmosphere—as dignitaries have freely come in and out of the capital. This kingdom-wide "open house" is capped off with a lavish banquet for the citizens of Susa who serve in the palace. It's a weeklong feast in the courtyard for the home folks, and the celebration is liberal. Even the normal protocol of drinking when the king drinks—and therefore not drinking when he doesn't—is lifted. Everyone can drink as much as he wants.

Queens normally don't attend such licentious affairs—it wouldn't be dignified or appropriate—so Vashti has a banquet of her own. It's more understated and less reckless, but it's interrupted by an unprecedented request. The king would like to show off his queen—apparently unveiled—to all the guests, both the high-ranking advisors and the servants, most of whom are inebriated. Persian women don't show themselves like that. Persian *queens* certainly don't shame themselves like that. It's a disgraceful request coming from a man drunk on his own power and glory, as well as his wine. The queen says no.

That's unprecedented too. Both the request and the refusal are shocking, and something has to give. The queen's dignity has been assaulted; the king's pride has been attacked; the royal standoff has to have consequences. In a monumental exaggeration, the king's advisors suggest that Vashti's noncompliance will spark a feminist movement in all the households of the empire. She must be made an example. The king disowns her as his queen, and she will never enter his presence again. And in an act of strength that does nothing but highlight his weakness, Xerxes issues a decree that women in Persia must respect their husbands.

Discuss

- What do the events of chapter 1 reveal about Xerxes as king? About the Persian culture Jews are living in? What challenges would a faithful Jew face in such a society?

  _____

  _____

  _____

  _____

A Quest for a Queen: Esther 2:1–14

Xerxes has been off at war—a failed attempt to conquer Greece—since his six-month festival for the country's leaders. In fact, the extended banquet may have involved some planning for that campaign. Now four years later, he returns home in defeat, and the memory of his banished bride only heightens the king's loneliness. He needs a new queen, and his advisors have a plan for how to get one. An empire-wide beauty contest should certainly harvest an appropriate companion for the king.

Young Jewish girls don't dream of being taken unwillingly into a pagan king's harem. It may be seen by some upper-class Persians as a privilege, but it poses all sorts of moral and ethical dilemmas for a woman of God. And even beyond morality, there's little appeal in being tried out for one night by a king and, if rejected—or simply forgotten—resigning oneself to a life of probable celibacy within the palace. There's no option of marrying someone else and no chance of becoming queen once

JUDAISM'S UN-JEWISH BOOK

Not only does Esther make no mention of God, it also contains no references to prayer, Jewish dietary restrictions, Jewish feasts from the law of Moses, or laws or traditions about intermarriage with foreigners. In this regard, it is highly unlike its relative contemporaries—such as 1–2 Chronicles, Daniel, Ezra, Nehemiah, Haggai, Zechariah, and Malachi—all of which emphasize themes important to the post-exile restoration of Jewish law and worship (including the temple) in Jerusalem. It is a book by a Jew for other Jews who are still scattered abroad and living in pagan societies.

someone has been chosen. Harem members may only wait to be summoned, and not all of them are. Few could consider that a fulfilling way of life.

Yet that's the apparent fate of a young Jew named Hadassah. The family tree of her and her relative Mordecai is traced back to the father of King Saul of the tribe of Benjamin, a lineage that will prove significant in upcoming events. Her Persian name is Esther—it comes from the goddess Ishtar and means "star." She is taken into the harem and begins the yearlong royal treatment of oils and lotions, cosmetics, and a special diet. The harem manager notices her and gives her extra attention. And Esther is able to have at least limited contact with Mordecai, the man who helped raise her after her parents' death. Mordecai has access to the courtyard and is often mentioned as being at the palace gate, a building used for administrative and judicial purposes. As someone with an official, palace-related position he can keep an eye on Esther. But he has told her not to reveal her ethnicity. Why? Perhaps he knows his penchant for protest could cause trouble for her later, or maybe the seeds of anti-Semitism are beginning to grow in Persian society. Regardless, it's best that she not be open about her background. Being a Jew offers no advantages in the king's harem.

Discuss

- Some people see Esther as compromising her faith by fitting smoothly and quietly into the harem—she offers no Daniel-like protests against Persian ways, for example—while others see her secrecy and compliance as godliness. Which do you think best fits the story? How would you have responded if you were in her situation? As Christians, how do we decide when to go along with the world's systems and when not to?

_____

_____

_____

_____

God's People in Place: Esther 2:15–23

Esther has won the favor of the harem manager, and now she will "try out" for the position of queen by spending a night in the king's bed. It's one of several uncomfortable chapters in the life of Esther. Not many years later, Ezra and Nehemiah will try to purify Israel of mixed marriages by forcing Jewish men to divorce the pagan wives they had brought back to the Promised Land (Ezra 10:9–11; Neh. 13:23–27). Nevertheless, Esther is cooperative with this unsavory process and the possibility of her union with a thoroughly pagan monarch. The result of her compliance and her beauty is great esteem in the eyes of the king. She becomes his queen four years after Vashti was rejected. The king and the kingdom celebrate.

In the course of his official palace duties, Mordecai overhears an assassination plot against the king and sends a warning through Esther, who duly gives him credit for uncovering the scheme. Mordecai's name is written in the king's annals, and the schemers are executed. Their bodies are impaled on a stake—many translations call it a "gallows," though its purpose is simply to display corpses as grotesquely and humiliatingly as possible and to deny the guilty ones a proper burial. It's a graphic warning to any would-be perpetrators. And while these criminals hang on display, Mordecai becomes an official hero in the royal records.

Discuss

- What cultural differences do you think Esther and Mordecai had to overcome to show such strong loyalty to Xerxes' reign? In what ways does their example apply to Christians living under governments they disagree with?

  _____

  _____

  _____

  _____

A CASE STUDY

Imagine: You had such dreams for your life—the career you wanted to have, the sweetheart you wanted to marry, the place where you wanted to live. But while vacationing on a remote island nation in the Pacific, the island's government is overthrown in a sudden and decisive coup. The new government, a thoroughly totalitarian and isolationist regime, has no plans to allow people off the island, regardless of their citizenship. Your government has demanded the release of its citizens, of course, but there are only three of you, and the State Department says that "no military response is required at this time." While slow diplomatic measures proceed, you are ordered to work in a labor camp, forced to marry a local spouse, required to live in an obscure village, and prohibited from practicing your faith. As far as you can tell, you are there to stay. And there's nothing you can do about it.

- What would happen to your relationship with God if you were forced into this system that rearranged all your plans and dreams? Would you see these events as God's will or not?

- How long would it take you to accept your circumstances and perform the duties of your job and marriage to the best of your ability? Would you ever try to fit into your new life?
- Why do you think Esther accepted her lot in life with a seemingly positive attitude? How hard do you think it was for her to do that? How hard would it have been for you?

When Crisis Strikes

ESTHER 3

Today we call it "ethnic cleansing," a sterile sort of term only a little less blunt than "genocide." But it still evokes gruesome images of mass graves and scarred societies. In some places, like the killing fields of Cambodia, the destruction has been more ideological than ethnic. But in places such as Rwanda, Bosnia, and Darfur, it has shown up as a brutal conflict between people of differing genealogies. It's always "us" versus "them": good guys and bad guys, Hatfields and McCoys, Capulets and Montagues. Only in cases of ethnic cleansing, the conflict plays out on the much larger scale of a region, a country, or even a continent or an empire. Regardless of the size of the stage, the tension between the actors is the same. Two people from different sides of the conflict are instant enemies—just because of who they are.

Such is the case with Haman and Mordecai, two of the key players in the story of Esther. They may not know each other personally, but their lineage from centuries past makes them instant enemies. Both men emigrated far from their homeland and live in a Persian capital city, but ancient hostilities transcend borders and eras. Haman and Mordecai are ethnic and religious rivals.

Such conflicts seem primitive and barbaric to those of us who live in a culture that values tolerance above practically any other virtue. Ethnic hostility is always a threat to a melting-pot society. And though our modern sensibilities—and the gospel of Jesus, for that matter—try to build bridges and establish unity among diverse peoples, God has often taken sides in conflicts of this world. He has never declared one ethnicity better than another, but he has drawn clear distinctions between those who are his people

WHY HE STOOD

Contrary to popular belief, there's nothing in Hebrew Scripture that would have forbidden Mordecai from bowing to Haman. Bowing to worship anyone or anything other than God is forbidden, but bowing to show honor or respect for someone is not. Abraham bowed before the Hittites (Gen. 23:7, 12); Jacob bowed to Esau (Gen. 33:3); Joseph's brothers bowed to honor him as a ruler of Egypt (Gen. 43:28); Moses bowed to his father-in-law (Exod. 18:7); and Nathan and Bathsheba bowed to David (1 Kings 1:23, 31). So why didn't Mordecai bow to Haman as a sign of respect? Because he didn't respect him. And, as Mordecai explained to the other officials, he was a Jew. Clearly this was ethnic hostility from the beginning—a fact that helps explain the intensity of Haman's rage.

and those who are not. And when a conflict arises between those who are his and those who aren't, he does not remain neutral.

That's a comfort for us. We need to understand, of course, that God wants everyone to be one of his people. Anyone who repents and turns to him is never turned away. But when we find ourselves in conflict with an anti-God world or its ungodly systems, we know we have an Advocate and a Defender. In any situation in life, we can ask him to save and know that in one way or another he will.

An Age-Old Grudge: Esther 3:1–6

Long ago, as Israel came through the Red Sea and into the wilderness, an army of Amalekites attacked God's chosen people. In one of Israel's most grueling battles in Scripture, Joshua's army fought well as long as Moses's staff was raised high but began losing whenever Moses lowered his arms. With some help from Aaron and Hur, Moses kept his arms up until Joshua secured the victory. The battle was won, and God vowed to wipe the Amalekites from the earth (Exod. 17:14; Deut. 25:19). They were designated for destruction.

Hundreds of years later, Israel's first king was given an assignment: attack the Amalekites and wipe them out (1 Sam. 15:1–3). Saul defeated the enemy but spared Agag, the Amalekite king. Samuel remedied the situation—he executed Agag himself—but it's clear that Saul let other Amalekites live too. They multiplied and continued to be a thorn in Israel's side for centuries to come. They came to represent Israel's unfinished business in the Promised Land.

In a far-off land much later in history, the Israel-Amalek rivalry flares up again. Five years after Esther's marriage to the king, Xerxes has elevated one of his nobles to the rank of a prime minister. This official is named Haman, and he is described as an Agagite—a descendant of the same Amalekite king that Saul failed to destroy. Saul's unfinished business has come back to haunt the chosen people. Amalekites have persisted throughout the centuries. Now one of them is Persia's second most powerful man.

But Mordecai, a descendant of Saul's kin, will not bow to Haman. That's a risky stance, not unlike Vashti's refusal to come to Xerxes' banquet. After all, the king has ordered allegiance to his right-hand man. But Mordecai daily refuses to give honor to a long-standing enemy of Israel. In spite of the risks, he cannot bring himself to bow. Haman is an Agagite, and Mordecai is a Jew.

Haman is furious, filled with "rage"—a word that in Hebrew (*hema*) sounds eerily like his own name. His ego has been assaulted by a mere Jew. He wants revenge, not only against Mordecai but against his entire race. Just as God once vowed to wipe Amalekites from the face of the earth for opposing Israel in the wilderness, Haman vows to wipe Jews from the face of the earth for opposing his power in a foreign land. Haman seeks to commit genocide.

Discuss

- Saul's failure to wipe out the Amalekites not only cost him his throne (1 Sam. 28:18–19), it plagued Israel for centuries to come. In what ways have you seen the long-lasting ripple effects of disobedience in your life or in the lives of others?

  _____

  _____

  _____

  _____

- God gave Israel several opportunities to make up for Saul's disobedience, and he will do so again in the book of Esther. In what ways have you seen him graciously provide opportunities to correct past wrongs in your life or in the lives of others?

_____

_____

_____

The Face of Evil: Esther 3:7–15

Haman casts lots to determine the most propitious day for destroying the Jews. While Haman is probably hoping for a date that's sooner rather than later, the lots (*pur*, or *purim* in the plural form) designate a date eleven months away. At least there's plenty of time for him to coordinate the pogrom. He begins to implement his strategy by seeking the king's endorsement.

To this point, Persian kings have been religiously tolerant. Xerxes' grandfather, Cyrus, allowed the Jews to return to Je-

ABOUT THE *PUR*

Casting the *pur* (plural *purim*) was like rolling dice. This was a widespread practice in most ancient Middle Eastern cultures, including Israel; it's referred to as "casting lots" in other parts of Scripture. Typically the person making a decision would ask a series of simple questions, cast the *pur* after each one, and trust divine intervention for the answers. Perhaps better than any other element in the story, the *pur* symbolizes the big question between the lines of Esther: is life a matter of chance and/or fate, or is a sovereign hand behind it? Proverbs 16:33 articulates the biblical answer: "The lot is cast into the lap, but its every decision is from the LORD." This is an unstated but pervasive theme throughout Esther's story.

rusalem, and his father, Darius, underwrote the rebuilding of the temple. That's because Persians have generally seen support of other religions as a way to build political support or at least to prevent unrest. But this decree is personal for Haman, and without specifying the Jews, he frames these despicable people in the most unflattering light. He convinces Xerxes that his own security is at stake. The king, ever malleable and easily influenced by his advisors, consents to the plan.

The decree is written on the eve of Passover, a holiday that celebrates God's deliverance of his people from an oppressive kingdom. It gives national militias, and apparently any citizens who want to join the melee, the authority to make a coordinated strike against any and every Jew. The agenda is exceedingly thorough: to "destroy, kill and annihilate" all the Jews—young and old, women and children—and to plunder their goods. Copies of the decree are made and distributed by couriers. And all the citizenry of Susa is utterly bewildered—literally agitated or disturbed—by the decree.

Discuss

- In what ways do you see God giving free reign to evil in Esther 3? In the world today?

  _____

  _____

  _____

- In what ways do you see God exercising control over evil in Esther 3? In the world today?

  _____

  _____

  _____

A CASE STUDY

Imagine: It may seem like something from a futuristic novel, but society really has changed in the last few years. Now in 2020, you find yourself in a brave new world—an era of new cooperation and peace and a high degree of social engineering. Your benevolent government leaders have come up with a solution for pesky problems such as food shortages and poverty but only because they are willing to make some hard sacrifices—"for the overall good of the people," of course. But you've just learned that people with your genetic history are being weeded out, or "cleansed," as the benevolent leaders prefer to say. In other words, to put it in archaic but very plain terms, you and all your relatives are among the many scheduled to be terminated.

- How would you initially respond to the threat of extermination? Would you protest or go into hiding?
- What would your relationship with God look like as the day of extermination approached? Would you pray in faith or lose heart? Would you perceive God as "an ever-present help in trouble" (Ps. 46:1) or a distant Master willing to let you suffer under his unyielding sovereign plans?
- Would your faith in God grow stronger or weaker during a time like this? Would you be drawn closer to him or be tempted to walk away? Why?

For Such a Time

ESTHER 4

Martin Luther had little idea when he protested the church's sale of indulgences that he would end up on trial for his life before an ominous assembly. The ninety-five theses he had nailed to the church door at Wittenberg, as well as his other writings, had spread quickly, thanks to the recent invention of the printing press. As a result, Luther's beliefs were widely known and had become quite controversial. Four years after his famous ninety-five theses, Luther was called to stand before a committee that he knew, in all likelihood, would declare him a heretic and possibly sentence him to death.

Even so, Luther appeared in the city of Worms having been promised safe passage to and from the city but with no assurances thereafter. He was questioned about his beliefs and whether he still held to the teachings in his books. Luther could have recanted and walked away freely, but at this critical moment in history—though he could not have known how critical at the time—his resolve remained firm. He declared that he could not go against his conscience and retract his statements. And, in the same spirit as Esther's famous statement "If I perish, I perish," he is said to have uttered these landmark words: "Here I stand. I can do no other. God help me. Amen."

God has a way of putting his people in crisis moments that turn the tide of history in the direction he wants it to go. With Luther, the already scattered seeds of reform burst into full bloom, and the Protestant Reformation spread too widely to ever be stamped out. With Esther, the tenuous position of Jews throughout the Middle East was solidified and strengthened to an unprecedented degree. In both situations, the catalyst is forced into a precarious situation, and undoubtedly they would have preferred to avoid the discomfort. Nevertheless, God defended them and resoundingly vindicated them for all of history to witness.

ESTHER GROWS UP

Esther is a compliant character in the first four chapters of the book. She follows Mordecai's instructions faithfully, enters the king's harem without complaint, and carries out her queenly duties quietly. But Haman's decree marks a turning point in her life. After initially resisting Mordecai's plea to intervene, she accepts her role in the situation as a personal responsibility and then gives Mordecai instructions about coordinating a fast. From this point forward, she is no longer portrayed as the ward of her guardian or a pawn in the hands of the king; she is the catalyst for all of the momentous events to come.

Few of us are ever thrust onto history's stage quite as dramatically as Luther or Esther, but God still places us in critical moments when we have to put our beliefs on the line or step up to the calling we've been given. Sometimes we're well aware of those moments; other times we only recognize them in retrospect. Regardless, we need to be ready for them. We need to live with the kind of faith that makes us available at any time for any purpose God has in mind, even if (perhaps especially if) he puts us in a situation that makes us tremble.

The Threat: Esther 4:1–11

Some people accept the destiny handed to them. Others challenge it. Mordecai falls into the latter category, and he begins by lamenting vocally and demonstratively along with quite a few other Jews—a sight surely pleasing to Haman. The king's edict is a baffling tragedy in every corner of the kingdom. Mordecai will make sure it gets negative attention.

Insulated within the palace walls, Esther is unaware of political rumblings outside. But she does hear that her cousin Mordecai is in deep distress and has adopted the behavior and clothing of a mourner. She dispatches a servant to find out why he is so grief-stricken, and Mordecai sends him back with the whole story, complete with insider details and a copy of the decree itself. Mordecai also urges Esther, via the messenger, to plead the case of the Jewish people. No longer is she to keep her ethnicity a secret. It's time to stand up for her people.

Esther is reluctant. It's a dangerous matter to approach the king uninvited; some people have lost their lives doing just that. She can't assume that she will have a chance to mention the situation to Xerxes the next time they are together—it has been a month since he last called for her, and there's no guarantee he

31

will summon her anytime soon. Mordecai must not understand the gravity of what he is asking her to do.

Discuss

- How do you respond when you receive bad news that seems beyond your ability to change? How do you view God for allowing those situations? How difficult is it for you to trust that he is in control over your circumstances? That he will respond to your prayers for his intervention? Why?

_____

_____

_____

_____

The Opportunity: Esther 4:12–17

Mordecai responds to Esther's predicament. Perhaps she doesn't understand the gravity of the situation outside the palace. He's certain that God will preserve a remnant of his chosen people somehow, but Jews in Susa—including the one inside the palace—may not survive this decree. Perhaps this is Esther's moment in history, the reason she had to go through the dehumanizing process to become royalty five years earlier. Will she seize the opportunity?

Yes, she says. But not without knowing her people are behind her. She asks Mordecai to organize an emergency fast—absolute abstinence from food and drink for three days.. She and her maids will do the same. At the end of the time, she will defy the law and put her life on the line. If she and her people are going to die anyway, she might as well die trying to save them.

Discuss

- When any group faces a crisis, there are two types of people that may be observed: those who watch for others to step up with a solution and those who feel responsible to step up with a solution themselves. Which response seems most natural to you? Which do you think was most natural for Esther? What aspects of the situation compelled her to get out of her comfort zone?

_____

_____

_____

A CASE STUDY

Imagine: You're faced with a huge decision at one of life's forks in the road. You've asked God for guidance, but he hasn't given it yet. Now the deadline for making a decision has arrived. If you could see all the pros and cons clearly and know how each option would play out, the decision would be easy. However, you can't see into the future, and from here both options look equally good. Once you've made the choice, there's no turning back. To choose one is to eliminate the other.

- How much pressure do you feel to "get it right"?
- How confident are you that God will guide you into the right decision? Why? If you end up making a decision without a clear sense of guidance, would you second-guess yourself or move forward trusting God's sovereignty?
- In what ways do you think God compensates for us if we "miss" his will in crisis moments?

33

A Model of Intercession

ESTHER 5–6

There were two outs in the bottom of the ninth inning of the seventh game of the World Series. The home team was down by two runs with the bases loaded, and the city held its breath—especially when they realized that their last hope for a comeback sat squarely on the narrow shoulders of the shortstop, a great fielder with less-than-stellar batting statistics. As several hundred million people around the world watched, the batter stepped into the box to face the league's best relief pitcher. Some hitters relish such moments; others get sick to their stomachs. This one fell into the latter category. Everything—the team's chances of victory, the city's hope, his own place in history, and perhaps even his career—was on the line.

Everyone can relate to the stress of make-or-break moments filled with pressure, nervousness, and a pounding heart. For some people, it's a tryout or interview for the team, school, or career of their choice; for others, the stakes are much higher, and the fate of a movement or a country rests in their hands. Crisis situations can be overwhelming. We wonder why we got ourselves into such predicaments in the first place, and we want to get through them as quickly as possible.

Esther's heart must have been pounding when she stood in the king's court. She knew the possible outcomes, and some of them were frightening. The worst-case scenario would have been rejection, a death sentence, and the loss of her people's only spokesperson within the palace walls. She also knew there was a chance of great success; that's why she was there. But she had to feel a sense of dread over what might happen.

God gives grace and courage for such times. Even when we feel like we're going through a crisis all alone, he's there to orchestrate events and influence hearts. No situation is beyond his control.

Make-or-Break Moment: Esther 5

The thought must have crossed Esther's mind: *The former queen was told to come into the king's presence and refused, and now she's gone. Now I'm going into his presence without being invited at all, and what will happen to me?* It had to be a nerve-racking moment. With the designated date of destruction still months away, we might wonder why Esther doesn't wait a bit longer to see if the king will request her presence again. Or why she doesn't simply try to arrange a visit with him through normal procedures. Would she have to arrange such a visit through Haman—and therefore have to explain her reasons for wanting to see the king? Perhaps. Regardless, this has become the moment of decision. She enters the court with her life on the line. Will the king raise his scepter? Or will she die?

The scepter is raised. The king is pleased to see her and generously offers to answer whatever request is on her heart. But Esther doesn't tell him. Not yet. First she must set the right mood. She invites Xerxes and his right-hand man to a banquet.

The king accepts. Esther must make preparations—Persian banquets are lavish affairs with plenty of servants and musicians and wine. But during the wine course, when the king again asks Esther what she desires, she hesitates. Is she being coy in order to pique his curiosity? Is she nervous about the fact that he's drinking wine, just as he was doing when his temper flared at the last queen? Or is she just nervous because of the magnitude of her request? Whatever the reason, she defers with an invitation to another banquet the next night. She will answer the king then and make everything plain.

Esther doesn't realize that while she is hesitating, Mordecai is in urgent danger. Haman leaves the banquet in great spirits, but his mood is ruined when he sees the Jew who dishonors him at the king's gate. Haman's *hema*, his rage, boils again. He calls together his friends and his wife so he can boast to them of all his

ESTHER THE INTERCESSOR

Many have seen Esther as a symbol of intercessory prayer. She went to the king and received an extravagant invitation to ask, even though he could have rejected her simply for approaching his throne. Likewise, we have no inherent rights to enter God's presence, but he figuratively lifts his gold scepter to us and invites us to confidently approach the throne of grace (Heb. 4:16). With this picture in mind, consider the repeated opportunities Esther is given to ask freely for anything. In 2:13; 2:15; 5:3; 5:6; 7:2; 8:4; and 9:12, the king urges her to request whatever is on her heart.

wealth and favor; apparently his ego needs some stroking because one Jew won't bow. His bitterness has greater power over his soul than his blessings. His wife suggests that he build an enormous stake, ask the king for Mordecai's execution, and then humiliate the corpse by hanging it for all to see. Then he can enjoy the next banquet in peace. Haman is delighted with the plan.

Discuss

- Why do you think Esther put off her request twice? What thoughts might cause you to put off a huge decision or a critical moment?

  _____

  _____

  _____

  _____

- Why do you think Haman's bitterness toward one person prevented him from enjoying "his vast wealth, his many sons, and all the ways the king had honored him" (5:11)? Do you tend to focus more on the ways God has blessed you or on the ways life isn't working out as you had hoped? In what ways do these attitudes compete against each other?

  _____

  _____

  _____

  _____

A Twisting Plot: Esther 6

Esther's hesitation turns out to be the key chronological feature in the story. After the first banquet, Xerxes has a sleepless night.

37

ENORMOUS GALLOWS

Persians didn't execute people by hanging. The "gallows" was actually a stake on which already-executed bodies were impaled and displayed for their public humiliation. The suggestion that a structure seventy-five feet high was built for the execution of Mordecai is considered by many commentators to be an enormous exaggeration—and clear evidence that Esther is a farcical piece of fiction. The tallest building in Susa was no more than three stories—roughly thirty feet high—which makes a structure more than twice that height seem implausible. It's possible, however, that the designated height was intended to portray the gallows being strategically placed on a wall or hill in an elevated part of the city—that is, seventy-five feet above the surrounding ground level. In other words, hang his body at the highest possible place so that everyone from miles around will see his shame.

He passes the time with some night reading—the annals of his reign. When the foiled assassination plot from several years before is read to him, the king wonders what was ever done to honor Mordecai. A long-forgotten good deed is remembered at the most opportune time.

At the exact moment the king is wanting advice about how to honor Mordecai, Haman arrives to request Mordecai's execution—though neither man mentions the Jew's name. In a tragically humorous misunderstanding, Haman suggests that the honoree—himself, he thinks—should be given the royal robe, placed on a royal horse that wears the royal crest, and be led by royal princes throughout the city while loud declarations of honor are shouted for all to hear. He is essentially suggesting kingship for a day and, perhaps in his mind, the status of heir to the throne. And shockingly, Xerxes agrees to such pomp—for Mordecai.

The humiliation is unbearable. Haman must orchestrate the extreme display of honor that he had desired for himself and give it instead to his archenemy. His downfall has begun. He is in an irreversible process of becoming the poster child for Proverbs 16:18: "Pride goes before destruction, a haughty spirit before a fall." And his wife sums up one of the book's dominant themes: "Since Mordecai . . . is of Jewish origin, you cannot stand against him—you will surely come to ruin!" (6:13). Before Haman has time to respond, he is hurriedly ushered to the banquet Esther has prepared.

Discuss

- Several verses in Scripture say that "God opposes the proud but gives grace to the humble" (James 4:6 and 1 Peter 5:5 quoting Prov. 3:34). How has this principle played out in Esther 6? How have you seen it at work in your life and in the lives of people around you?

  _____

  _____

  _____

  _____

A CASE STUDY

Imagine: For a remarkable two minutes, God allows you to see and speak with the angels he has assigned to guard you. Part of your initial shock is due to the fact that you're actually seeing angels, but part of it is due to their enormous power and size. You ask them what their specific orders are, and their leader informs you that God has declared you a watershed figure for

39

the people around you. Whoever blesses you will be blessed, and whoever curses you will be cursed. Whoever opposes you, regardless of their strategies and tactics, will be defeated. In fact, any attempt to harm you will backfire and cause you to become stronger.

- How confidently would you go through life if God made that declaration about you?

- How well do you think this scenario depicts the statement Haman's wife made about the Jews (6:13)? How accurately do you think it depicts God's promise to all who believe in him?

- In light of the obvious fact that godly people do experience hardship, suffering, and death at the hands of adversaries, what relevance do you think this biblical principle has today? In what sense are we protected and preserved by God?

Reversal

ESTHER 7–8

The emperor forced the young Skywalker to look out the window and observe the destruction. The Rebel Alliance had been drawn into a trap, and the evil Empire's forces were picking off Rebel ships one by one. The weapon systems of the unfinished Death Star were fully operational and much more powerful than the Rebels had thought. From all outward appearances, the Empire was about to completely wipe out the ragtag Alliance. The desperate fight against evil was about to end in disaster.

Those familiar with *Star Wars: The Return of the Jedi* know, of course, that good stories don't end that way. As Luke Skywalker lay helpless under the "Force lightning" streaming from the emperor's fingers, Darth Vader took pity on his son and threw the emperor into a chasm. Meanwhile on the moon Endor, the

41

Rebels disabled the Death Star's shields, allowing Rebel fighters to fly into the battle station's inner piping and trigger a massive explosion to destroy it. In a matter of moments, what looked like certain doom turned into decisive, permanent victory. And the celebration on Endor—old Jedis appearing and smiling from beyond the grave, Ewoks drumming and cavorting, and hugs and kisses among all who fought so valiantly—was a picture of wild and unrestrained exhilaration. Mourning had turned to dancing in a hurry.

God's stories about his people don't end in disaster either. Many may die in the fight, but the victory always comes. He knows how to turn ashes into beauty and mourning into dancing, and sometimes he does it with the suddenness of a lightning strike. No situation is too desperate for God, no crisis is too severe. He is always working in and through situations to accomplish the best for his people in exactly the right timing.

This is true for us collectively as the body of Christ and for each of us individually. Whatever we go through, no situation is too urgent. God is never late, even though he stretches our sense of timing beyond what we think we can bear. Though he often takes an excruciatingly long time to set up key events in our lives,

SIGNET RING

Some have seen Esther as a Christ figure—an intercessor who identifies with both the God/king figure and the vulnerable masses destined for destruction, and who sacrificially steps in to plead the case for salvation. In this light, the king's handing of the signet ring to Mordecai because of Esther's mediation takes on profound significance. It points forward to a time when Jesus would grant a share of his authority to his followers and authorize them to pray and minister in his name (Matt. 10:1; 16:19; 28:18–19).

when he acts, he can dramatically change circumstances with startling speed. That's what he did with Haman's plot against the Jews, suddenly reversing the fortunes of Haman and Mordecai and securing the place of Esther's people in the kingdom. And that's what he often does in our times of crisis. We never have reason to lose hope. Our circumstances, no matter how frightening or desperate, are never beyond his reach.

An Enemy Undone: Esther 7

At the second banquet, Esther finally voices her petition. Her life is in danger, she explains, as are the lives of her entire race. They "have been sold for destruction and slaughter and annihilation" (7:4). She is careful with her words—they must vilify Haman without accusing the king for his part in the decree. So in extremely humble, unassuming language, she begins pointing a finger at the yet unnamed offender.

Xerxes asks none of the exploratory questions that might be expected: "Who are 'your' people? What decree are you talking about? Who is designated for destruction in my kingdom?" Perhaps he puts the facts together between the verses of this chapter, or perhaps he is unconcerned with the details. Either way, his queen's life is threatened. He wants to know only one thing: who's behind it.

This time, Esther doesn't beat around the bush. She pointedly identifies Haman as a vile enemy. Again, Xerxes doesn't try to sort out the facts. He seems to know she is right. He storms out in a rage, and Haman, in a gross breach of protocol, stays in the room with the queen. Being in her presence when the king is not in the room is, in itself, enough to get him executed. But he takes it further. He pleads. He even falls on the couch where she reclines.

43

The king walks in on this most unseemly picture, and Haman's fate is sealed. His head is covered in disgrace, he is immediately executed and hung on the gallows, and the king's fury subsides. In a matter of days, Mordecai has gone from sackcloth to royal robes while Haman has gone from royal robes to an execution cloak. The tables have completely turned.

Discuss

- Are there any difficult situations in your life that you want God to suddenly reverse? What does the book of Esther say about his ability and/or willingness to do so?

_____

_____

_____

- How long had God been working on the "sudden" reversal of Esther's and the Jews' situation? Is it encouraging to you in your times of crisis that he laid the groundwork for a solution well ahead of Esther's crisis? Why or why not?

_____

_____

_____

Mourning to Dancing: Esther 8

The king has rights to the property of those who have been executed, so he confiscates Haman's estate and allows Esther to appoint Mordecai to keep it. Xerxes also gives Mordecai the signet ring once worn by Haman—a scene reminiscent of Joseph and Daniel, both of whom rose to high office in foreign courts—making him the kingdom's new second-in-command.

But the threat to the Jews isn't over. The king's edict is still in effect and must remain so. Royal decrees cannot be revoked. While there's no historical record of a law in the Persian Empire that prevents revoking a decree, it may have been a tradition kings employed to save face and appear decisive. Regardless, it's the reason Xerxes gives for not pulling the plug on Haman's plot. But he does have a possible solution. Mordecai can write another decree in the king's name that will allow Jews to form militias to defend themselves on the day of destruction. They may do to their enemies exactly what was planned for them without any repercussions.

The city that was "bewildered" and deeply disturbed in 3:15 now holds a "joyous celebration" (8:15). Throughout the empire, Jews rejoice along with many who align themselves with the Jews. The "mourning," "fasting," "weeping," and "wailing" in 4:3 are replaced by "happiness," "joy," "gladness," and "honor" in 8:16. The wrongs proposed in the first half of the book are now being reversed in the second.

Discuss

- The book of Esther portrays a sudden reversal from mourning to dancing in the lives of Mordecai and the Jews. In what ways have you seen God turn grief into joy in your life or in the lives of people you know?

_____

_____

_____

_____

A Case Study

Imagine: After years of faithful service, a series of misunderstandings at work caused you to lose your job. It was bad enough that the circumstances worked out as they did, but when your boss explained why you were being let go, it became clear that a coworker had been manipulating the situation for some time, lying about your contributions to various projects and about how "difficult" you are to work with. Over time, you were unfairly but consistently portrayed as the reason for delays and sloppiness. And not knowing how your reputation was being tarnished, you were unable to defend it. By the time you were let go, it was too late.

But within a month of your being fired, your boss sees the truth of the situation, realizes you weren't to blame, and rehires you in a different position—one that is more suited to your interests and abilities and that comes with a 30 percent salary increase. Your "downfall" had set the stage for your promotion. You couldn't have worked it out better if you had tried.

- In the month between being fired and being rehired, how much would you have appreciated God's sovereign will? In the battle between faith and bitterness in your heart, which attitude would have had the upper hand?

- How would you perceive God's sovereign will after being rehired? To what extent would you have been able to thank him for having been fired?

- How difficult would it be to live in gratitude for God's rescues and provisions before they actually happen? In what situations have you seen the "gallows" in your life—your apparent downfalls—as symbols of your eventual triumph?

A Testament to Triumph

ESTHER 9

It was one of the worst seasons of Joan's life, and the longer it lasted, the more discouraged she got. The pressure was almost unbearable. Why wasn't God working to resolve the situation? Why were answers to prayer so long in coming? Come to think of it, why did God always seem absent in hard times? Where was the help so emphatically promised in Scripture? Joan could remember dozens of unanswered prayers compared to only a handful of answered ones. The more she thought about it, the more distant God seemed.

While looking through a stack of papers one day, Joan came across her old journal. Flipping through the pages, she was surprised to see all the check marks she had put by her prayer requests to indicate that they had been answered. As she read how God had dealt with her in past crises—and realized that she had come through them much stronger and better established than she had been before—she began to realize how distorted her current perspective was. She had been looking at God through the lenses of her discouragement and forgetting how faithful God had always been.

That's easy to do when we go through difficulties. We tend to magnify our immediate problems and lose sight of the big picture. The problems of today look like mountains, and the victories of the past look like molehills. We begin to question God's faithfulness and wonder why he isn't paying any attention to us. Our crises appear huge, and our God seems small.

That's why celebrating God's past work in our lives is so important. It brings the memory of his power into our present circumstances and builds our faith. We pray with more confidence when his past mercies are in the forefront of our minds. We go through difficulties with a deeper assurance that he will eventually bring us out of them—and that he will use the entire experience for his greater purposes and our greater good. Though a big-picture perspective doesn't make our trials go away, it does make them a lot easier to bear. And we draw closer to God by remembering what he has done.

The last chapters in Esther were written for just that purpose: to forever remind Israel of how God had defended them. The themes of this book would be important to remember in numerous dark periods of Jewish history as well as in the individual lives of every one of his people. Connecting with the past has a dramatic impact on the present and the future of those who live by faith.

From Defense to Offense: Esther 9:1–15

"The tables were turned" (9:1). One of the major themes of Esther is fulfilled when the enemies of the Jews have to go on the defensive because of all the public sympathy for a race that was slated for destruction. The Jews strike down all their enemies—at this point, probably only Amalekites and other dyed-in-the-wool anti-Semites—and also put an end to Haman's family line. They honor a commandment that Saul had neglected to fulfill centuries before. And as part of that original command, they refuse to lay hands on the plunder. They obey in all the ways their first king didn't.

Esther presses for more—another day to accomplish the task and permission to display the dead sons of Haman. The king again gives her whatever she wants, though this time he seems surprised that she could want more than he has already given. Nevertheless, he consents. The extension applies to the city of Susa only, giving Jews time to finish their business in the place where the plan to exterminate them was first hatched.

TURNABOUT

The theme of "turnabout" or sudden reversals is a prominent feature in the book of Esther. The word that describes how the tables turned in 9:1 is the same word used in Deuteronomy 23:5 for God turning Balaam's attempted curse into a blessing for Israel and in Psalm 30:11 for God turning mourning into dancing. It describes a decisive, complete switch from one extreme to the other. God's ability to reverse a threatening situation and use it for good is also reflected in the life of Joseph (see Gen. 50:20) and in Romans 8:28—as well as in the lives of many people throughout history and today. The glimpses of this dynamic that we get in Scripture and in our own lives point to the ultimate turnabout described in Revelation when Babylon is judged in a single hour and the bride of Christ is revealed.

Discuss

- Centuries before Esther, God had issued both a promise and a command for the Amalekites' destruction—neither of which seemed to have an expiration date. In what ways does the perpetual nature of his promises and commands encourage you? In what ways does it challenge you?

  _____

  _____

  _____

  _____

Remember: Esther 9:16–32

The conflict between Jews and their enemies outside of Susa is confined to a single day, the thirteenth of Adar, which is followed by a day of rest and celebration. In the capital, however, the conflict lasts for two days and is followed by a celebration on the fifteenth. Mordecai and Esther formalize these celebra-

UNCHANGEABLE DECREES

The idea of a decree that cannot be revoked comes up twice in Esther, both with Haman's plot and with Esther and Mordecai's reversal. But this policy has never been found in Persian documents. It may have been a well-known but unwritten legal requirement, or it may have simply been a common practice to prevent the king from appearing weak and losing face. From the portrayal of Xerxes in Esther—as a king with absolute power who has trouble making his own decisions—it's reasonable to wonder if he was trying to compensate for his frequent wavering by appearing resolute with every decree.

tions into an annual holiday—two festive days each year to remember "when their sorrow was turned into joy and their mourning into a day of celebration" (9:22). This holiday—called "Purim" for the *pur* that was cast to decide their fate—is to be celebrated throughout all future generations to remind Jews of God's extraordinary favor on his people and his ability to give them victory over any enemy.

Discuss

- In what ways have you seen God turn negative situations into positive blessings in your own life or in the lives of people you know?

  _____

  _____

  _____

  _____

- Why do you think it's important to remember the victories God has won for us? How do past victories relate to present crises? What effect does remembering have on our faith? What specifically do you think God wants you to remember about the ways he has worked in your life?

  _____

  _____

  _____

  _____

A CASE STUDY

Imagine: It was the most desperate prayer you had ever uttered, and God came through for you. It may not have seemed like that big a deal to outside observers, but to you it was huge—a major miracle. It was clear evidence that God was listening to you, that he was concerned for the things on your heart, and that he was on your side. When you needed him most, he gave you a dramatic victory. And you'll forever be thankful.

- In what ways would you commemorate and celebrate such clear evidence of God's faithfulness in your life? What would you do to make sure you never forget?
- In what situations would you find it most encouraging to recall the great victory that God gave you? How would it build your faith for your prayers today and in the future?
- What specific events in your relationship with God currently perform this encouraging role? What specific practices would you be willing to adopt today to help you remember and celebrate God's goodness?

Conclusion

Celebrated in late February to mid-March, the feast of Purim is Judaism's most joyous and festive holiday. Throughout history, rabbis have urged reckless frivolity in the celebration. During Purim services, the entire Esther scroll is read from beginning to end, and the congregation supplements the reading with hisses and boos and noisemakers at every mention of Haman's name. And when the rabbi reads the list of Haman's ten sons in chapter 9, he recites the list in one breath—as though he can't wait to get through the names of such enemies.

But the book of Esther is more than an explanation of one holiday's origins. It's a story of how God took something Satan meant for evil and turned it around for good. It's true that neither God nor Satan is mentioned in the book, but nearly every reader in Judaism and Christendom sees them both clearly at work in the story. And when seen as a glimpse of the cosmic conflict between the Creator and his enemy, Esther becomes much more than one episode in Israel's history. It becomes a snapshot of the message of the entire Bible.

Think about it: Haman's thirst for power, honor, and worship has a lot of similarities with the appetites of a certain angelic being described in Isaiah 14 and Ezekiel 28—passages heavy with symbolism of Lucifer's fall. On a stage much bigger than Haman's, Satan planned a "gallows" for the defeat of Jesus and determined to have him hung on it. But that instrument of defeat has become the ultimate symbol of victory over death and the grave. The enemy was completely undone by the cross, and his perceived authority as "the prince of this world" (John 12:31; 14:30; 16:11) immediately gave way to the one who declared, "All authority in heaven and on earth has been given to me" (Matt. 28:18).

In a sense, the Gospels portray a role reversal between the humble Son of Man and the proud deceiver. That reversal also applies to the church at the end of the age, when the accuser of God's people will be hurled down (Rev. 12:10) and believers will be raised up to rule with Jesus on his throne (Rev. 3:21; 5:10; 22:5). The Hamans of this earth and the unseen realms will fall, and the meek will inherit the kingdom, just as God demonstrated in the ancient kingdom of Persia.

The book of Esther is a significant episode in biblical history. It shows us that the weapons raised against God's people will not prosper; that God is willing to intervene in our lives no matter how desperate our situation is; and that even when he has not made his name obvious in our story, we can still see him with the eyes of faith if we'll read between the lines.

Leader's Notes

Session 2

A Case Study. This scenario will undoubtedly seem far-fetched to group participants, but it would hit close to home for any Jew in Esther's day or during World War II, for the persecuted Christians of the early church (such as James, Peter, and the believers gathered at Mary's house in Acts 13), for many twentieth-century Christians in places such as the Soviet Union or China, and for believers in some countries today. In other words, the situation isn't nearly as far-fetched as it seems. Many of God's people in various eras have gone through quite similar circumstances.

Session 4

Esther 6, discussion questions. Scripture is emphatic about this principle. God hates pride and is drawn to humility. For further examples, see Psalm 138:6; Proverbs 15:33; 16:5; 18:12; 22:4; 29:23; Isaiah 2:11–12, 17; 57:15.

A Case Study. God essentially made this promise to Abraham and, by extension, to his physical and spiritual descendants throughout the ages. It's obvious, however, that this promise applies in ultimate terms and not always in immediate terms. Abraham's descendants do suffer defeat. The discussion should honor both the realities of life in a fallen world and the inviolable truth of God's promise to defend his people. An in-depth discussion of what Genesis 12:3 and Esther 6:13 mean—and what they don't mean—can reveal a variety of interesting perspectives among participants.

Session 5

Esther 7, discussion questions. Obviously, the book of Esther is not a guarantee that God will reverse every painful or difficult situation we face—though it does indicate that he is always watching out for his people. Even so, Esther provides a model for prayer and hope in dark times. Help participants see their part in the equation; we can humbly petition as Esther did, stand confidently in the face of a crisis, and then trust God to deliver in his way and in his time.

Esther 8, discussion questions. Just as the biblical theme of pride going before a fall is graphically portrayed in Esther, so is this theme of "mourning to dancing." It may be helpful to read Psalm 30:11 and Isaiah 61:3. The first passage is a psalm of David, the second is a messianic prophecy. This may be a good opportunity for group members to tell personal stories of God turning mourning to dancing or bringing beauty out of ashes—and to encourage those who are struggling through the first part of that process and need hope for how it will end.

Session 6

Esther 9:1–15, discussion question. If group members need any prompting, directly ask what specific promises have yet to be fulfilled in their lives and encourage them to see those promises as permanently valid. Also ask what specific commands they have yet to follow in their lives and encourage them to see those instructions as permanently valid.

Bibliography

Berlin, Adele, Marc Zvi Brettler, and Michael Fishbane, eds. *The Jewish Study Bible*. Oxford and New York: Oxford University Press, 2004.

The Five Megilloth, vol. 1: Esther, The Song of Songs, Ruth. New York: The Judaica Press, 1992.

James, Carolyn Custis. *Lost Women of the Bible*. Grand Rapids: Zondervan, 2005.

Kaiser, Walter C., Jr., and Duane Garrett, eds. *Archaeological Study Bible*. Grand Rapids: Zondervan, 2006.

Kee, Howard Clark, Eric M. Meyers, John Rogerson, and Anthony J. Saldarini. *The Cambridge Companion to the Bible*. Cambridge: Cambridge University Press, 1997.

Reid, Debra. *Esther: An Introduction and Commentary*. Downers Grove, IL: IVP Academic, 2008.

Ryken, Leland, and Philip Graham Ryken, eds. *The Literary Study Bible*. Wheaton, IL: Crossway, 2007.

Telushkin, Joseph. *Biblical Literacy: The Most Important People, Events, and Ideas of the Hebrew Bible*. New York: William Morrow, 1997.

Walton, John H., Victor H. Matthews, and Mark W. Chavalas. *The IVP Bible Background Commentary: Old Testament*. Downers Grove, IL: InterVarsity Press, 2000.

Helping people everywhere
live God's Word

For more than three decades, Walk Thru the Bible has created disciple-ship materials and cultivated leadership networks that together are reaching millions of people through live seminars, print publications, audiovisual curricula, and the Internet. Known for innovative methods and high-quality resources, we serve the whole body of Christ across denominational, cultural, and national lines. Through our strong and cooperative international partnerships, we are strategically positioned to address the church's greatest need: developing mature, committed, and spiritually reproducing believers.

Walk Thru the Bible communicates the truths of God's Word in a way that makes the Bible readily accessible to anyone. We are committed to developing user-friendly resources that are Bible centered, of excellent quality, life changing for individuals, and catalytic for churches, ministries, and movements; and we are committed to maintaining our global reach through strategic partnerships while adhering to the highest levels of in-tegrity in all we do.

Walk Thru the Bible partners with the local church worldwide to fulfill its mission, helping people "walk thru" the Bible with greater clarity and understanding. Live seminars and small group curricula are taught in over 45 languages by more than 80,000 people in more than 70 countries, and more than 100 million devotionals have been packaged into daily maga-zines, books, and other publications that reach over five million people each year.

Walk Thru the Bible
4201 North Peachtree Road
Atlanta, GA 30341-1207
770-458-9300
www.walkthru.org

Read the entire Bible in one year, thanks to the systematic reading plan in the bestselling **Daily Walk** devotional.

The **Daily Walk** devotional magazine includes book introductions, charts outlining book and chapter themes, and background information on each day's reading. Insightful observations shed light on the culture, the history, and the context of passages. Each daily reading is loaded with helpful applications that enable you to apply biblical truth to your life. Readers are sure to find the time they spend in the Bible more productive and rewarding than ever before.

Ideal for church-wide or group Bible study, bulk subscriptions to **Daily Walk** offering significant savings can be purchased online at www.walkthru.org. Discounted individual subscriptions are also available online.

WALK
THRU THE
BIBLE®

www.walkthru.org
Individual Orders: **800-877-5539**   Bulk Orders: **800-998-0814**